HAIKU HUES

ANAMIKA MITRA

INDIA • SINGAPORE • MALAYSIA

ISBN
Paperback 979-8-89632-402-7
Hardcase 979-8-89632-807-0

For

Atisha and Manavendra
My children
Sparkle Happiness Inspiration

Foreword

If poetry is the art of expressing the deepest emotions in brevity, Anamika's book would fit this description to a T. She, in her debut collection (Haiku), writes about everything that catches her attention.

The reader would be pleasantly surprised that these are things and thoughts that they themselves have had, somewhere in their years on this motley planet of ours. A Haiku, as a form, requires the highest expertise in creating meaning for a reader from the three lines which they have as a form to express what otherwise would take pages. Anamika, through her deft pen, creates moments of epiphany, as her Haikus seem familiar to the reader. This is because she writes about the ordinary and transforms them into an experience extraordinaire.

Whether reflecting on the master's love for his pet and the reciprocal, or in these lines; "How much do we need?/Quench your thirst and control greed/Limit the unlimited". The contrast in her range of emotions may be witnessed where, on one hand we have the highest emotion of love, be it for an animal or pet and the unlimited nature of man's greed. This exposes the heart of the poet, a heart that thinks…reflects on those thoughts and expresses them in words that would befit a master. When she writes "There is no blueprint of life…", we understand, because of the nature of human life, which is at best, fickle. Some of her writes make us stop for a moment before the flooding realization of her depth in meaning hits us. This can be seen in her writes like; "Minus one/Plus one/Happy birthday." Here the very condition of human life, aging, is considered into three lines of expression that makes us think and arrive at a realisation.

In truth, Anamika seems to have been writing for a long time because her expressions are of someone who is familiar with words. This familiarity comes only with having been in association with words, through voracious reading and through penning down your thoughts. For the reader, this is a collection that will remain with them for a long time. In fact, I am sure they would be forced to return to it, to pick it up again, whenever a question or a situation compels them. Anamika has done well in making this whole collection a gift for the astute reader, for the lover of words and for the common man. She writes, not as a writer but as a person creating a craft. She crafts each thought of hers into treats for the senses.

Dr. Arunav Barua (Poet, Author, Acadamic)
Assistant Professor, NERIM Group of Institutions,
Guwahati, Assam.

Introduction

Haiku Hues

This Haiku collection is my first time attempt to pen down life's observations in three line format. Somewhere between aging and maturing certain incidents and observations hit hard. Expressing them through long pages would be burdensome in the already tightly hectic schedules of ours. Herein, popped the idea of experimenting with Haiku. Though not strictly following the 5-7-5 format, what I have done is stick to the three lines. I hope critics will excuse my liberty. In the spirit of free writing with an open mind I have jotted the haikus without any intentional damage/harm to any type/ structure/ sentiments.

The haikus are about the ordinary observations and feelings. These are nothing out of the world. Contrarily the themes are present around us. They are so common that we do not even notice them. I hope these haikus will make the dear readers notice the little things that otherwise goes unobserved.

I have included a few of my sketches for pictorial impact and this being another form of human expression though I humbly acknowledge that I am a dilettante.

I am grateful to my poet friend Dr. Arunav Barua, who suggested that I publish these Haikus. He even spared his valuable time to write the foreword and I am thankful for having such a comrade.

I am thankful to my children, Atisha Mitra and Manavendra Mitra, who are my constant support and source of unwavering love.

I also thank my upbringing in the continuous loving support of my parents, Lt Sushil Chandra Mitra and Smt. Biju Mitra, who made me able enough to go through ups and downs while staying grounded and relating to the ordinary mundane matters and affairs of life. Staying closer to the grounds keeps us sane and stable in the fast life of our times.

I am thankful to the supportive team of Notion Press whose professional guidance made the publication possible.

Over and above I keep faith and hope high even during times of crisis which makes me express the hues of life in a precise focused form without frills of fancy and whim.

Anamika Mitra

18.11.2024

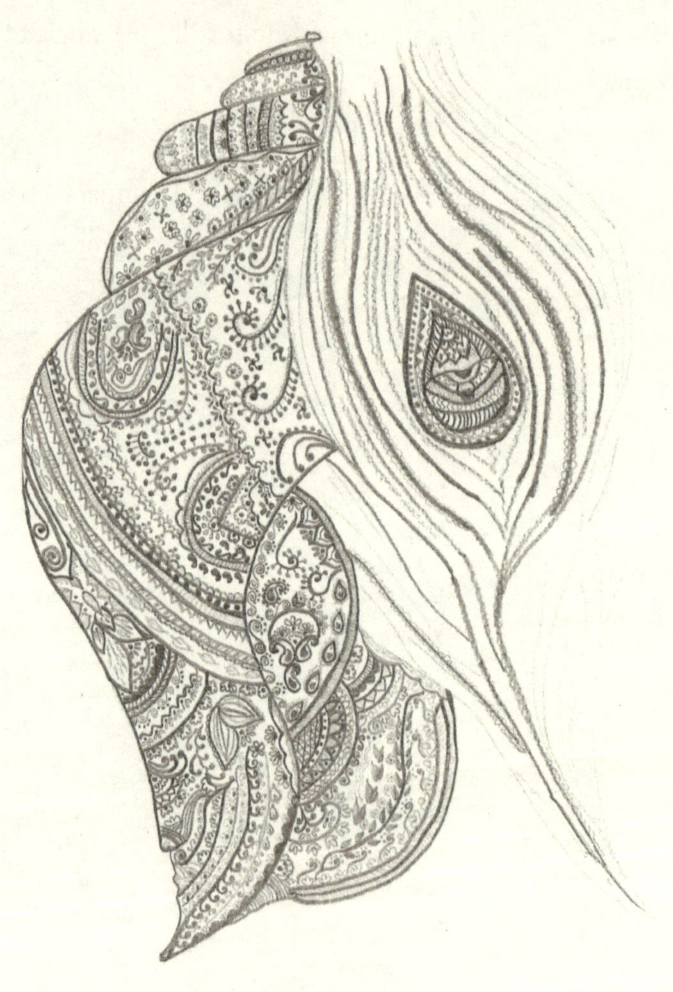

A/M 2024

Two chuckling pigeons
Sitting along the roof silt
Lovebirds cooing…

Telescopic lake side

The old wooden lonely bench

Spotted a couple

Eiffel tower

Versailles grounds

Lido steals the show.

Green foliage
Turning yellow and orange
It becomes fallen

Pair of swans swimming
Elegantly gliding through
Still water rippling…

Fragrant new book

Crisp pages unturned

Waiting for eyes…

The husband names

The wife recalls as whose name

And then both forget

Curled cat

Wafting fishy aroma

Cozy bed empty

Dog waggles

Master wriggles

Loyal love

Lady in goggles

What is she hiding?

What is hidden from her…

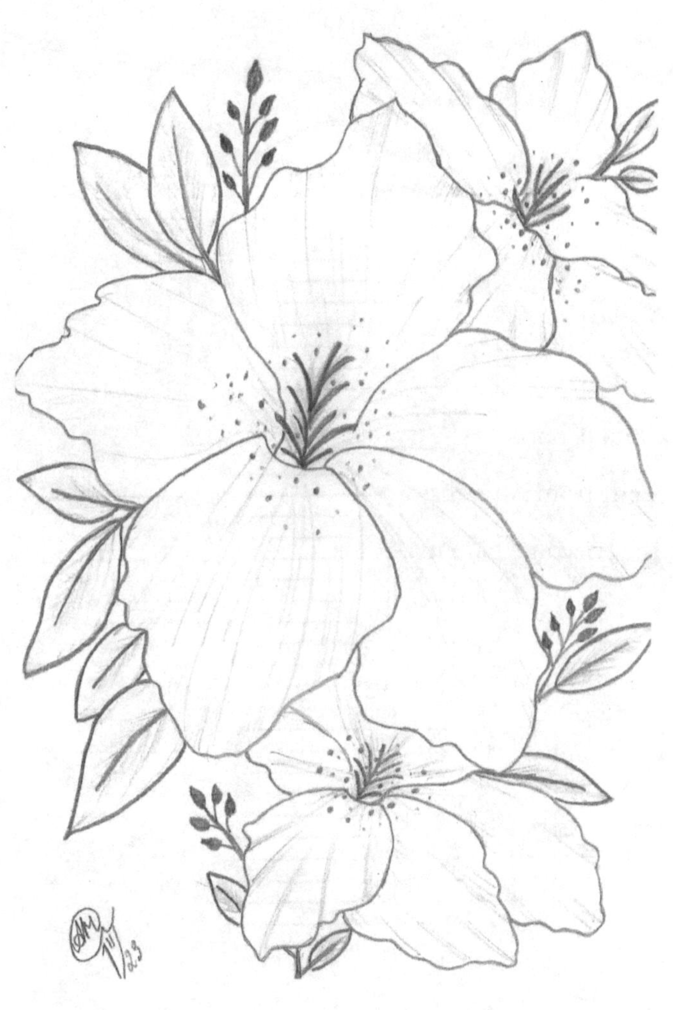

Child is born
A gift from Almighty
They become parent

She smiled at him
His heart melted like cheese
And he smiled back…cheese

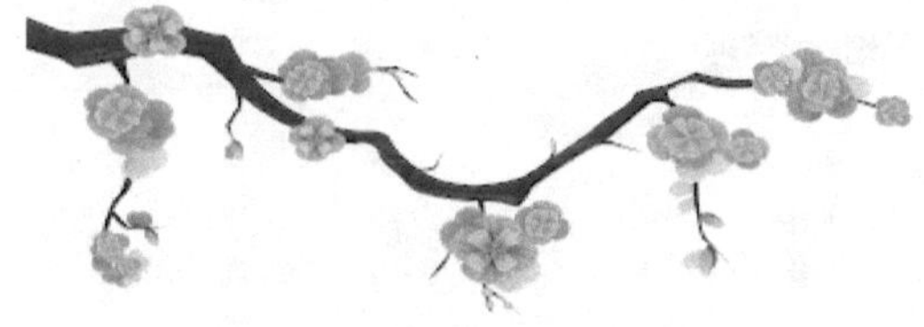

She held his hand

He pressed hers

A moment of cosmic connection…

I looked up at the night sky
Full moon and starry
But my eyes teary…

Traffic point
A junction of signals
Direction in three shades

Tea served in porcelain cups

Delicate cutlery

Delicate leaves left to soak in hot water

Cafeteria it is
Tables occupied, not full
Whiff of grounded beans

How you see the sunlight

It burns and scorches bright

Lo! it gives the heat and warmth to survive

The moon is smiling
So is the woman on earth
A phase of stages

4/2020

Night sky twinkling stars
Gradually curtained clouds
Moon peeps and smiles

Boys on beach
Playing with the ball
The setting sun slowly sinks in the horizon

Lovely lady

Who has named you so?

The lover or the betrayer

I am the king, so he proclaimed

I am the queen, she wanted to pro/claim

The crown choose, but only one!

You said you loved her
But she could never see nor feel
Only hear loud empty words…

He took her softly
Treated her gently
Loved her purely

Temple with long queues
Devotees with offerings
Awaiting divine interaction

Pray in silence
Chant in your mind
Recite aloud

Auspicious day – the main door

Garland of marigold flowers

Mango leaves with sindoor dots…

He promised her a world
She believed
He finished the 'she' in her

Updated profile picture

Directed and intentional

Lack of courage – camouflaged-coward

Status update

Share or propaganda

Let the viewer decide…

Facebook post
Mundane or not
Private made public…

Make no plans

Everything is permanent when alive

Everthing becomes temporary when living through

There is no blueprint of life
The earthquakes and tsunamis of mind and body
Shakes and stirs us constantly

A dreamer and charmer of things and possessions
You create illusion to play your games
Lest the Magician bares it all

Praying everyday
Connecting with the Almighty
Bonding through believe and faith

Clock strikes midnight

Woke up with a jerk

Did I lose my slipper?

Magpie pair perched on the branch

A sign of happiness

A symbol of joy

Green parrot camouflaged in a gulmohar tree
Parroting the coy girl humming underneath
Unaware and oblivious

The cat cat-walking the tin roof
A mouse was heard squeaking
As the old bolts on the tin roof loosened.

The beautiful green valley
Overlooking the vast expanse
Far away a tiny yellow glow flickers

Early winter mornings
The warm blanket hugs tightly
Doesn't want to fall apart

Winter noon

Feel the sweet sun kissing

The juicy orange quenching the thirst

Gradually sun spreads the rays
Afraid to cut the winter coldness
Still braves the hours to spread the warm rays

Composed a few lines
Thinking a poet is born
Each is an artist of sorts

Proud of self

But where shall this end

The end is just a goodbye

You said, I believed

You behaved, I saw

Vice versa – Understood

Highway toll gate measures and counts
Payments decide continuity of journey
But the roads connect even without

They crossed paths again

He smirked at her

She failed to understand why a stranger smirked at her

He wrote to her about love

She knew he was playing

Decades later she proved intuition is never wrong

She calculated her giving

God counted His blessings

She lost count of her calculations.

Surprise, surprise, surprise
This is life
Surprise surprise and more…

Planned one life

Lived a different life

Dreaming of another life

Strokes on canvas
Splashes of colors
Art exquisite

Meeting room – heated chillness

Divided in opinion

Debating for consensus

Lawyer's desk

Gentlemen or criminal

The black coat

Spring colors

Red and yellow

Passion and prosperity

Holding hands
Without movement or sweet words
Silence speaks

Soft breeze of emotions

Scented winds of change

Love unleashed

Teenage girl
Soft sweet delicate
Determination and grit

Season of spring

Life blooming and love growing

Time of surrender

Nurse station

Constant attention

Duty call

Luminous sky opens up

Earth is prepared and ready

Pre-plan

Empty canvas
Brushed in varied hues
An impression imprinted

He smiles

Pecks a kiss

She blushes surprisingly

Tiffin box

Flavors packed to full

Hunger nourished and appeased

He sings a song

She dances attuned

They thus play

To live casually
Yet life is a formality
Complete confusion

My thoughts

My lines

Overlap and negates

A studded red bag full
In a long flight of longings
Flaring and raging

He looked lovingly
She too plunged in the sweet depth
Loved and locked forever.

Moon full and bright
Lover amazed and dazzled
Reminiscing his beloved.

High sea roars and grumbles
In acceptance or rejection
High handedness of Mother Nature

Home coming

Everyone was eager and happy

But left only yesterday

The maiden on the 18th floor
Waiting for reality to brush her cheeks
As the cool breeze moves past.

Solar eclipse

Light and shadow plays

Solar spectacle.

a/m 2023

Minus one

Plus one

Happy birthday

Tiny and fragile
Drunk with sweet nectar
The honeysuckle

Grandson screams

Grandma rushes

Mother sits and watches

Curtain ruffles
Sound of soft steps can be heard
Curtain pulled aside.

Setting sun

Woman widowed

The sinking red dot

Full moon

Encircled flawless beauty

Awaiting to reflect

Hospital bed

What use is power and wealth

I cannot barter death.

The sweet smile is gone
Replaced by overthinking
Worthless crippling thoughts.

Another summer day

Unbearable heat

How real is global warming?

Nature nurtures all
Yet man wants to have it all
Giving versus greed.

The woman howls

Neighbors sighs and grieves for her

She is but madness.

How much do we need?

Quench your thirst and control greed

Limit the unlimited

The old man wakes up
Remembers nothing but all
Forget all yet none.

Baby crawls
Mother rushes to grapples
Innocent giggles

In the club they met

Over tennis and by the pool

Karaoke at lounge.

Moulin Rouge Paris
Casinos and clubs at Vegas
Home is to return.

Wine and cheese
Tastebuds tingling
Truffles scheming

Coffee house

The aroma and smoothness

Expresso.

Love is pure

Love is sacred

Can love be forbidden

Day breaks over the serene hills
And a whole path lies ahead
Marking destiny

Paris in my mind

London New York and Vegas too

But never was it you.

Constantly consistent
Always in flow
Mighty Brahmaputra

Rays peep through
On the dewdrops
Prism without rainbow

It's my life
And today I am alive
So let's live it up tonight.

About the author

Anamika Mitra, a gold medallist in Political Science and a law graduate, has experiences as - lawyer, lecturer and writer (academic and non-academic). An entrepreneur hailing from the northeastern city of Guwahati in the picturesque state of Assam, she has travelled extensively across the world since a very tender age. An avid reader, swimmer, and traveller, she is self-taught in sketches and culinary innovations alongside creative writing, especially in the form of poetry. Having also spent many years outside Guwahati has given her an insight on the vastness of space and the limitations of time. The exposure to multiple tiny experiences that are otherwise personally deeply emotional has been translated into various forms of expressions. Having already published two collections of poems—Folks of Nature and Illusion of Being, this is her first attempt with Haiku. Currently, she lives in Guwahati and communicates through her esteemed readers via WhatsApp #94355-55836 or via email: mitra18anamika@gmail.com.

www.ingramcontent.com/pod-product-compliance
Lightning Source LLC
LaVergne TN
LVHW091104150826
845673LV00002B/715

* 9 7 9 8 8 9 6 3 2 4 0 2 7 *